CCHS #3951-910

W9-AHA-374

CCHS #9848-393

anew the familiar story of the founding of the town and the steady development of the community. Local leaders proposed erecting a steel tower and observatory and building a road for automobile access. They contacted James Welch, then residing in California, about use of his property. The Centennial Committee erected a huge sign, illuminated at night with electric bulbs reading "1811-1911." Although the road project was beyond reach, John Friend Chitwood, then in his 70s, cleared a four-foot-wide trail up the southwest slope of the ridge. Chitwood had promoted the idea of a three-story observatory with lighted tower to commemorate the explorers Meriwether Lewis and William Clark. He perceived the monument as a "guiding star for the mariner upon the Pacific."

The most important consequence of the 1911 centennial was that events generated surplus money, including funds donated by John Astor, a descendant of fur trader John Jacob Astor, for whom Astoria was named. The Centennial Committee and the Park Commission decided to use these funds to buy land on Coxcomb Hill for a park. In 1914, the City of Astoria purchased 30 acres at the summit. The new Astor Park attracted speakers, singing events, and picnics. With the coming of World War I and a wave of patriotism, the aged John Chitwood advertised for two able men "with inspiration in their souls and the ability to perform" to climb and cut the limbs from a 90-foot tree on the hill.

Joean K. Fransen, historian of events at Coxcomb Hill, wrote about the labors of Otto Pestila, a 34-year-old Finnish American who carried out Chitwood's scheme: "In driving winds and pelting rain he worked long hours with practiced skill and proven confidence. Using spikes driven into the trunk as steps, he worked his way up the tree. At the top he made a platform of a few snags into which he wedged an 80-pound bronze ball, a must for the top of a flagpole. Then he reefed a steel halyard through the pulley, trimmed the platform and climbed down, cutting the branches as he descended." On July 4, 1917, Chitwood raised the Stars and Stripes, while down in the town the band played "America"

CCHS #3454-910

Top: Astoria looking east with Coxcomb Hill on the right
Above: Commercial Street and 14th Avenue, Astoria, 1923
Left: Booth Fisheries in Astoria, 1912

and "The Star Spangled Banner" and patriotic speakers addressed the contributions of trader and explorer Captain Robert Gray, Lewis and Clark, John Jacob Astor, and the pioneer settlers.

Gradually Coxcomb Hill—which probably took its name from the court jester's cap adorned with a fake rooster tail—had become an important part of civic pride in Astoria. The town's residents, having acquired it for a park, cleared part of the ridge and used it for events. In 1923, the City Council revoked the permit for operation of the stone quarry in the park. Then, on December 7, lightning struck the flagpole, setting it ablaze and ending another chapter in symbolic use of the site.

Although several individuals and groups floated proposals to erect a landmark on the hill, nothing jelled beyond the short-lived centennial sign and flagpole-tree. In 1922, the core of the city had been swept by a devastating fire that destroyed much of the commercial district and a number of residences. This staggering blow fostered a determination to rebuild and led to the construction of a number of handsome buildings including Hotel Astoria, a new City Hall, and the Liberty Theater. In 1924, Mrs. R.E. Barrett, city manager of nearby Warrenton, proposed a monument on Coxcomb Hill to honor Lewis and Clark. In 1925 Thompson Coit Elliott, a regional historian, concluded that the park was an ideal site for a memorial to Captain Robert Gray, explorer of the Columbia River. The Astoria Park Commission agreed. City officials considered constructing a 40-foot viewing tower, but took no action.

"

When I first conceived the idea of a memorial of some kind on Coxcomb Hill, I hadn't the slightest idea that today we would be looking upon such a column as stands before us."

Ralph Budd, quoted in *The Oregonian*, July 25, 1926

A memorial was a fine idea, but would be costly to build and maintain. Coxcomb Hill needed a champion with both vision and resources.

RALPH BUDD AND THE GREAT NORTHERN RAILWAY

Between the 1830s and the 1920s, railroads made significant profits hauling freight and passengers. Ralph Budd (1879-1962) was a premier promoter of railroads and tourism. In the mid-1920s Budd grasped the potential of tapping history to promote travel. A man ahead of his time in embracing heritage tourism, Budd sought ways to educate the general public about American history while laying the groundwork for excursions on the Great Northern Railway to sites he had identified and helped elevate to symbolic importance. Budd embraced history with great passion. The warmth of his personality and his drive were often mirrored in his projects. He was able to convince others to dream his dreams and "get on board."

NEWBERRY LIBRARY

Ralph Budd

A farm boy born in Iowa, Budd completed high school and college in six years, graduating with a degree in civil engineering. Initially employed by the Chicago Great Western and then Rock Island railroads, Budd confirmed his early promise and found himself under the tutelage of John F. Stevens, a prominent railroad engineer. At age 27, Budd joined Stevens in the Panama Canal project. Budd's success in constructing a modern railroad across the Isthmus of Darien attracted the attention of James J. Hill, principal owner of the Great Northern Railway, who hired the young man. One measure of his abilities is that in 1919, at age 40, Budd was named president of the Great Northern.

Budd realized the importance of passenger traffic to the financial success of the Great Northern. The railroad ran not only through rich agricultural regions but also through the Rocky Mountains and the Cascade Range in Washington. Hundreds of miles of the route afforded vistas of stunning beauty but did not produce products—nor did towns line the tracks. Budd knew that the scenic beauty along the route could attract travelers. The Great Northern had had considerable success in building hotels and promoting Glacier National Park as a tourist destination. In the mid-1920s, he focused on history as a new magnet for tourism.

The timing was right. Americans had become increasingly nostalgic about the development of their country. They had celebrated it in the Centennial Exposition, Philadelphia (1876); Columbian Exposition, Chicago (1892); Louisiana Purchase Exposition, St. Louis (1904); Lewis and Clark Exposition, Portland (1905); Panama-Pacific Exposition, Seattle (1915); and the Panama-California Exposition, San Diego (1915). Americans were also mindful of the passing of the generations who had emigrated in wagon trains to the West. The lore of the pioneer was vanishing. Some Americans hoped to capture, as Grace Flandrau, a friend of Budd's, phrased it, "a temperate and lovely land of legend," and help the pioneers "take an ever more significant place in the history and conquest of America."

In 1925, Budd conceived the Upper Missouri Historical Expedition. He invited approximately 125 historians, cultural leaders, and boosters of communities in several Western states to book passage on the Great Northern to visit sites of historical events. Budd wanted to commemorate figures who had opened up the American West for "civilization." Mitigating the ethnocentrism of his program, he included participation of Native Americans at several points in the agenda.

The Upper Missouri Historical Expedition left Chicago by train in July 1925 to follow Budd's itinerary. At Verendrye, North Dakota, the participants erected a granite sphere to honor David Thompson, a British explorer, fur trapper, and geographer. They held a congress with eight Indian tribes at Fort Union, North Dakota, and visited the site near Havre, Montana, where Chief Joseph surrendered at the end of the Nez Perce War in 1877. They erected a granite obelisk to honor Meriwether Lewis's explorations

LANDMARK OF THE PACIFIC CROSSROADS

HISTORY HAS PLAYED OUT IN GRAND DESIGN IN ASTORIA, OREGON. THE FIRST PERMANENT EURO-AMERICAN SETTLEMENT IN THE PACIFIC NORTHWEST, THE COMMUNITY VAULTED TO SYMBOLIC IMPORTANCE IN 1811, WITHIN MONTHS OF ITS FOUNDING BY THE PACIFIC FUR COMPANY. INTERNATIONAL RIVALRIES REVOLVED AROUND THIS SITE AT THE MOUTH OF THE COLUMBIA RIVER AND, BETWEEN 1812 AND 1846, BROUGHT GREAT BRITAIN AND THE UNITED STATES TO CONFRONTATION AND THE BRINK OF WAR. ULTIMATELY DIPLOMACY PREVAILED, AND ASTORIA BECAME A PIVOTAL BARGAINING CHIP IN THE EMERGENCE OF THE UNITED STATES AS A CONTINENTAL NATION.

Forces of history sometimes inspire the development of symbols. The Astoria Column, atop Coxcomb Hill, is one of the largest and most potent symbols of American presence in the Pacific Northwest. It is a remarkable structure drawing on the imagery of classical Rome, stories of Native Americans and early Euro-American adventurers at the mouth of the Columbia, technology of 20th-century construction, and the talents of a remarkable artist. The column is also the product of the ardent promotion of commerce and travel by the Great Northern Railway, the aspirations of a town that wanted to become a world port, and the desire to affirm in a symbolic monument the course of history.

COXCOMB HILL

Coxcomb Hill provides majestic vistas of the countryside surrounding Astoria. It rises 600 feet above the south bank of the Columba River. To the west, Cape Disappointment, a dark promontory covered with spruce trees, guards the mouth of the river. Point Adams, a low, sandy spit, lies on the south side of the river entrance. Saddle Mountain, site of the nesting area of the mythological Thunderbird and point of genesis of the Clatsop and Chinook tribes, rises on the southern horizon. In 1841, James Dwight Dana ascended this peak and made the first paleontological collections in the region. To the north, the distant shore stretches from swampy lowlands along the Chinook River to Point Ellice and Grays Bay. This was the homeland of the Chinook Tribe, cousins of the Clatsops, who lived on the south bank. To the northeast is Tongue Point, a low body of rock covered with forest that juts into the Columbia. Far to the east rise Mount St. Helens, Mount Adams, Mount Rainier, and Mount Hood, prominent, snow-covered volcanoes of the Cascade Range.

In 1898, members of the Astoria Progressive Commercial Association considered the prospect of constructing an observatory on Coxcomb Hill to provide panoramic vistas of the mouth of the Columbia River. The dream was for an electrified tower to rival that erected by Gustav Eiffel in Paris. Charles W. Shively, son of the town's first postmaster, offered to donate five acres for a park on the ridge. James W. Welch, another landowner, offered seven acres provided the promoters produced definite plans and financial backing. Nothing more happened.

Coxcomb Hill took a different direction from a park when, in 1903, a quarry on its north side began mining building stones, some of which were used in 1910 in the construction of the town's high school. The dream of a park, however, persisted. Interest in public use of the hill grew as Astoria celebrated its centennial in 1911. Joseph Gaston's *Centennial History of Oregon, 1811-1911* discussed

"Almost a century ago, stunted, pioneer Astoria,
its original fur trade gone, perked up in 1874 and started
to grow into a colorful fishtown."

Walter Mattila, *Finns and Finnicans,* 1970

CCHS #97-23524

of the Marias River in 1806 and placed a bronze statue of John F. Stevens, Budd's mentor, at Marias Pass in the northern Rockies. The travelers met at Two Medicine Chalet in Glacier National Park to plan more expeditions exploring the history of the route traversed by the Great Northern. General Hugh Scott was elected president; Budd was honorary president; and Agnes Laut, historian of the fur trade in the northern Rockies, was secretary.

Budd intended to erect markers and monuments at a number of sites close to the route of the Great Northern Railway and its subsidiary lines. Emboldened by his success in attracting travelers to the cause, he announced plans for a projected Columbia River Historical Expedition during the next summer. In 1926, Budd outfitted a special train with a "Museum Car" containing exhibits, books, and photographs. The railroad sponsored a high school oratorical contest to assess "The French Pioneers in America." The student winners—5 from France and 38 from the United States—were invited as guests of the railroad for the 1926 expedition.

Following initial sessions in Chicago, the Columbia River Special departed on July 15 for St. Paul and points west. Lectures, parades, banquets, flag raisings, Indian dances, and songs educated and entertained the travelers. As the expedition traveled beyond the Rockies, Budd erected new historical symbols. These included a sandstone tablet com-

memorating the route of trade and travel across Idaho at a site near Bonner's Ferry; a basalt monument honoring pathfinders and Oregon Trail pioneers at Wishram, Washington; and a major monument to be dedicated on Coxcomb Hill in Astoria. At the mouth of the Columbia River, Budd planned the greatest symbolic statement in the United States to affirm exploration and early settlement in the American West. On the expedition's return, Budd dedi-

Wishram, Washington

Great Northern Railway station, Astoria, Oregon

cated the Spokane Plains Battlefield Monument. The travelers sojourned in Glacier National Park, and returned on July 27 to Chicago.

Budd had initially envisioned a large flagpole with a substantial base to stand on Coxcomb Hill. Through conversations with architect Electus D. Litchfield of New York City, however, he learned of Attilio Pusterla, an Italian artist who had mastered the craft of *sgraffito*, carving images in plaster. By December 1925, Litchfield projected a decorated column rising to 100 feet at a cost of $24,500. The column would commemorate Native Americans and the early history of development at the mouth of the Columbia River. Budd later said, "I have been given credit for the idea of the column, but this was Mr. Litchfield's idea–the architect."

DESIGNING THE ASTORIA COLUMN

Electus Darwin Litchfield (1872-1952) was a well-established architect in practice in the partnership of Litchfield & Roger, New York City. A graduate of Brooklyn Polytechnic Institute (1889) and the M.E. Stevens Institute of Technology (1892), Litchfield was an heir to a fortune generated by his grandfather, Electus B. Litchfield, who had been a partner with James J. Hill in building the St. Paul & Pacific Railroad from St. Paul to St. Cloud, Minnesota. Electus D.'s father, William B. Litchfield, helped build the railroad and, for a time, served as its general superintendent.

As an architect, Litchfield drew heavily from classical forms. In a 42-year career he designed numerous public buildings, residences, and monuments. Among Litchfield's most important buildings were the St. Paul Public Library, Kirk Hall on the campus of Macalester College, and James J. Hill Reference Library, St. Paul, Minnesota; the U.S. Courthouse and post office, Denver, Colorado; the Customs House, Albany, New York; the Masonic Temple, Brooklyn, New York; and the City Club at 800 Park Avenue, New York City. Litchfield was also a visionary planner; during World War I he designed Yorkship Village, an industrial town and "garden

"The work of preparing the summit of Coxcomb Hill to receive the historical monument to be erected there this spring by Vincent Astor and the Great Northern railway will be commenced next week."
Astoria Evening Budget, February 6, 1926

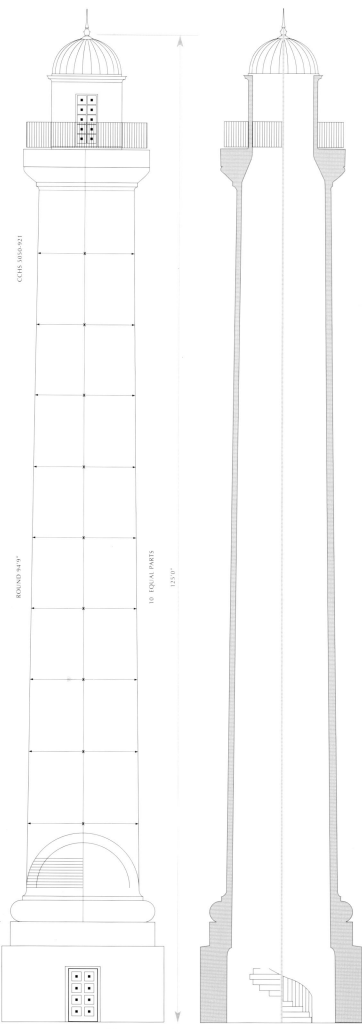

CCHS 5050-921

ROUND 94'9"

10 EQUAL PARTS

125'0"

The Astoria Column

© 1999 The J. Paul Getty Trust. All rights reserved.

Trajan's Column in Rome

city" for 1,700 residents near Camden, New Jersey, for the Emergency Fleet Corporation.

In the mid-1920s Budd employed Litchfield to design several monuments along the route of the Great Northern Railway. The Astoria Column– for its size and inspiration– became one of the architect's most notable works. Litchfield found inspiration in Trajan's Column in Rome and in the Vendome Column in Paris. Nearly 2,000 years ago the Roman Emperor Trajan com- missioned a *column cochlis*, a monument to celebrate his vic- tories in the Dacian Wars. The column, constructed of massive blocks of marble, rose to nearly 100 feet. Inside it a staircase wound upward, culminating at a viewing platform above a forum. This was a remarkable construction feat in the millennia before skyscrapers. More than 2,000 human figures at two-thirds life size, carved in circular bands on the exterior of the column, told of Trajan's military exploits. A monumental statue of Trajan on a horse stood atop the column. The Ven- dome Column, designed by the architects Denon, Gondouin, and Lepère and based on Trajan's Column, was erected between 1806 and 1810 in Paris. A spi- ral bronze bas-relief celebrating Napoleon's victory at Austerlitz decorated its exterior.

Litchfield seized upon the *column cochlis* for the memorial concept at Coxcomb Hill. The moment of epiphany–stepping out onto a small viewing plat- form approximately 110 feet above the ridge–would afford visitors a panoramic view of the edge of the North American continent, the broad Columbia River, and the majestic, snow-capped volcanoes on the east- ern horizon. The decorative detail for the exterior of the column would portray the stories of local Native Americans, explorations of sea captain Robert Gray,

"*Mr. Pusterla has his heart in his work, and they tell me that frequently he goes to work in the morning and chisels out something he has done the day before and does it over again, because when looking from the ground it has not satisfied him.*"

Ralph Budd, quoted in *The Oregonian*, July 25, 1926

the charting of the American West by Meriwether Lewis and William Clark, and the founding of Astoria by John Jacob Astor and his employees of the Pacific Fur Company.

CONSTRUCTING THE COLUMN

Events moved steadily after December 1925, when Ralph Budd announced plans for a monument. Astoria officials granted their consent. Vincent

Vincent Astor

Astor, great-grandson of John Jacob Astor, confirmed that he would join the Great Northern Railway in financing construction. In February 1926, bidders responded to the offering to clear the summit of Coxcomb Hill of vegetation, grade the site, lay out a permanent roadway, and prepare for construction. Integral to Litchfield's landscape plan was an oval around which he placed an encircling roadway, a series of platforms stepping up to the column's base, the column, and three concrete walkways radiating to the north, west, and south.

A.B. Guthrie and Company of Portland, the successful bidder, began work in March. The workers started by building the primary base platform, 19 feet 6 inches by 13 feet 6 inches, as a foundation. On it they constructed forms and poured concrete for the entrance room and shaft. The entry doors (replaced in the mid-1990s with replicas at both the ground and cupola levels) were in the Italianate style. The lower door has eight panels with brass studs, a central doorknob, and a side lever. Inside the shaft they affixed a circular iron staircase. In the cupola they placed a door with 10 panels and a side lever for latching. On top of the shaft the cupola was surmounted by a copper finial cap, 4 feet 6 inches tall, that extended over the viewing platform. The workers installed 15 curved-glass panels in the cupola. These were supported by 16 copper-flashed, wooden ribs attached to iron flanges bolted through a wooden collar into the column.

Construction moved rapidly. The column was ready for exterior decoration by late May, but the arrival of the Great Northern's Columbia River Historical Expedition in July proved premature. The artist still had much work to do.

The costs for the column were carefully itemized by the Great Northern Railway: $15,000 to A.B. Guthrie for construction, $2,875 to Portland Wire and Iron Works for the spiral stairway, $1,000 in architectural fees to Litchfield (plus travel costs), and $7,500 for the labors of the artist and artistic supplies. Of the total cost–$27,133.96–Vincent Astor donated $20,000. The Great Northern Railway picked up the additional costs and provided the services of A.J. Witchel, chief engineer of its subsidiary, the Spokane, Portland, and Seattle Railroad, to manage the project.

PUSTERLA'S CAVALCADE OF HISTORY

Ralph Budd hired Attilio Pusterla (1862-1941), an artist teaching in New York, to create a frieze and 525-foot-long mural to wrap around the shaft. An immigrant to the United States in 1899, Pusterla responded to the nationalism embraced by Americans following World War I. He designed boldly by finding symbolism in the deeds of heroic men (and a few women) who had helped the United States become a continental nation reaching from sea to sea.

Born in Milan and educated in Italy, Pusterla had studied with the Italian painters Cremona and

Attilio Pusterla

Giovanni Seggantini. In the 1880s he became a leader of the Revolutionary School of sunlight painters, who believed that works painted outdoors had more integrity and life than those done in a studio. Pusterla taught in the Leonardo da Vinci Art School in New York City and lived with his wife, Henrietta, in Woodcliff, New Jersey.

Pusterla's work in *sgraffito*, a technique known to Electus Litchfield, held promise as a means to

CORBIS

ASTORIA COLUMN OR ASTOR COLUMN?

"I think the official name 'Astoria Column' should be followed, especially as to call it 'Astor Column' would tend, I think, to emphasize the work of Astor and minimize Gray and Lewis and Clark."

Ralph Budd to Electus D. Litchfield, February 21, 1927

John Jacob Astor

portray the multiple historical events associated with Euro-American activity at the mouth of the Columbia. From Byzantium to Plymouth Colony, potters had used the technique for centuries. The potter crafted a ware, usually employing a dark clay, then applied a liquid slip in a lighter color. Using a spear-shaped blade, the potter then excised, widened, and deepened a decorative design, cutting through the slip to expose the darker under layer. The technique has also been used by children who lay down multiple layers of crayons and then scratch a design to reveal the underlying colors.

Sgraffito became a technique of considerable interest to late-19th-century designers and artists who embraced the Arts and Crafts movement. Working with different-colored layers of plaster, the skilled artist could produce in a relatively short time highly impressive murals and large wall decorations. Selwyn Image, Heywood Sumner, and Edward C. Burne-Jones became known for their work in *sgraffito* as well as in the technique of etching lines to make woodcut illustrations. Sumner employed *sgraffito* techniques to decorate 11 churches in Great Britain. Pusterla emerged in the early 20th century as one of the foremost masters of this art form in the United States.

During the spring of 1926 Pusterla worked on the designs. Anxiety mounted as the column neared completion and the artist remained in New York. The July 22 dedication date loomed, and the likelihood of finishing the commemorative story on its exterior on time receded. In May, Litchfield wrote to Budd:

> The minute that we got the approval of the sketches, Pusterla and his assistants started to work on making the cartoons. He had thought that he could save time by using photographic enlargements, but this did not prove to be the case and he is making them all by hand. I do not dare push him too hard for fear of making the aesthetic results suffer. He tells me it will be the end of June before he can finish all the cartoons.

The "cartoons" were the primary scenes to illustrate the historical narrative on the column's exterior. Their design was a critical step before the plaster could be placed and the views engraved in *sgraffito*. Pressed by both Budd and Litchfield to meet the dedication deadline, Pusterla wrote on May 20:

> I say that I am doing my best to rush work on the cartoons and will be ready to show some this week, if you let me know which day you prefer to come over to my house. . . . I have divided, the one inch to foot sketch, in 26 horizontal strips; the total length of the column being 89 feet, the full size cartoons are three feet and five inches wide. Work hard, as I am doing now, the average production will be four strips per week. I started on May 17, and to complete all cartoons without any interruption it takes till June 30th.

In spite of anxieties on many sides–among the officials of the Great Northern Railway, in leadership circles in Astoria, and in the construction team building the column–the artist did not arrive on site until the middle of June. The term "temperamental" appeared in more than one letter exchanged by those in charge of the project. Fewer than four weeks remained before the scheduled dedication ceremonies. Pusterla had taken nearly six months to conceive and prepare the sketches for the project. He and his assistants began work on July 1.

Gail Evans, author of the draft National Landmark nomination of the column, described some of the challenges the artist faced:

> Workmen constructed a donut-shaped, wooden scaffold for the artist, which hung by ropes from the column's 110-foot-high viewing platform. Each day Pusterla raised or lowered himself to work on the frieze. A small canvas tent suspended over the scaffold protected the artist from the inclement weather. Pusterla took his large completed cartoons up on the scaffold. After laying down the dark base coat, he placed the cartoon over the wet plaster. He then blew colored powder into holes poked in the outline of each figure. Lifting the cartoon away from the plaster, he could see the outline in powder. He then added the upper, lighter coat of plaster, and finished the image by incising shadows and outlines. Pusterla frequently chiseled away images from

Proceedings at
the Formal Dedication of the Astoria Column,
Erected in Honor of Robert Gray, Lewis and Clark,
and John Jacob Astor,
Through the Generosity of Vincent Astor.

His Excellency, Walter M. Pierce,
Governor of the State of Oregon, Presiding

Selections . . . Astoria Band *R. C. Cole,* Director

Invocation . . . Rev. E. A. Gottberg

"The Lewis and Clark Expedition"
. . . Major-General Hugh L. Scott

Vocal Selection . . . Astoria Chorus
Mrs. J. H. Shaner, Director

"Two Centuries of Oregon" . . . Dr. Samuel Eliot Morison

"New York and Astoria" . . . Lawrence F. Abbott

Response . . . Mrs. Richard Aldrich
Representing the Astor Family

Vocal Selections . . . Astoria Chorus
Mrs. J. H. Shaner, Director

*"Three Months, Residence at the
Columbia River, 1795-96"* . . . Judge F. W. Howay

*"Greetings from the New York
Chamber of Commerce"* . . . Howard Elliott

Selections . . . Astoria Band *R. C. Cole,* Director

Salmon Luncheon on Coxcomb Hill, Astor Park,
Given by Citizens of Astoria to the Members of the
Columbia River Historical Expedition

Above left: Astoria Column dedication, 1926. Oregon Historical Society Neg. No. 54023 *Right:* Program of dedication events, 1926

the previous day's work if he found them unsatisfactory after viewing them from the ground.

The dedication had to proceed without a finished monument. Pusterla and his assistants had completed only three bands of the great cavalcade of history.

DEDICATION OF THE ASTORIA COLUMN

The work atop Coxcomb Hill was still in progress on July 22, when an audience estimated at 8,000 assembled for the dedication. On that day the column suggested a giant umbrella stuck in the closed position, but nothing dampened the enthusiasm of those celebrating the culmination of Budd's 1926 Columbia River Historical Expedition. The travelers reached the Pacific Ocean on July 21 at Seaside with a tour of the "Salt-Makers Camp" of the Lewis and Clark Expedition. All had the option of an afternoon of golfing at courses in Seaside, Gearhart, or Astoria, or an automobile trip to Astoria for an afternoon parade. The following morning the Columbia River Special moved on to Astoria, where those aboard awakened in the rail yard.

Budd had recruited some of the most popular scholars on the region's early history. Judge F.W. Howay was a specialist in 18th-century maritime exploration. He edited the logs of Captains Robert Gray and James Colnett, wrote numerous historical articles, and coauthored *British Columbia from the Earliest Times to the Present* (1914). Samuel Eliot Morison was at the beginning of a long, distinguished career teaching at Harvard University, where he became well-known for his expertise in maritime and naval affairs; he also won acclaim for his biography of Christopher Columbus and a history of U.S. naval operations during World War II. Lawrence F. Abbott, a former aide to President Theodore Roosevelt, published his recollections as well as articles about Thomas Jefferson, Meriwether Lewis, and others concerned with the West in *The Outlook* (1926), of which he was editor. Abbott was president of the Franco-American Branch of the American Goodwill Association.

The dedication included many other events and participants: loggers displaying their skills at log-rolling, bathing beauties, a boxing match, aged pioneers, a flower show, five U.S. Navy ships, street dancers, bands, choirs, and the "Prunarians" of Vancouver, Washington. The City of Astoria stretched its events over three days. The city's "Spirit of the West" parade echoed in its floats and character actors a number of the subjects Pusterla was etching on the exterior of the great column.

When the tourists, local citizens, and special guests departed, the Italian-born artist resumed his labors. Weeks passed and bad weather dogged his efforts, but on October 29, Pusterla completed the colossal spiral mural. He had executed the first use of *sgraffito* on a monumental column. His artistry gave new identity to Coxcomb Hill.

DEPICTIONS ON THE ASTORIA COLUMN

THE MURALS ON THE COLUMN CELEBRATED THE EARLIEST MOMENTS OF THE HISTORIC EPOCH IN THE PACIFIC NORTH-WEST. NINETY-FIVE PERCENT OF THE IMAGERY DEALT WITH EVENTS BETWEEN 1792 AND 1818–PIVOTAL YEARS IN ASTORIA'S HISTORY. THE STORIES AFFIRMED THE IMPORTANCE OF THE

"Doctrine of Right of Discovery" championed by western nation-states. This doctrine used simple arguments to justify colonization of lands occupied by other peoples. Those of European ancestry, the reasoning went, possessed a settled agriculture, written languages, and Christianity. These were hall-marks of civilization, while the lands of hunting, fishing, gathering, non-Christian peoples without written languages were subject to appropriation and exploitation. Those of non-European ancestry were viewed as having a mere occupancy right to the land but no vested title.

Pusterla's murals subtly but confidently told the story of the dispossession of the Native American inhabitants of the Pacific Northwest. He reduced the Indians to a preface in the region's history. They occupied the forests and margins of the rivers and sea but played little role after the arrival of intrepid European and American explorers. The heroes in the murals were men of the late 18th and early 19th centuries who were driven by the quest for profits through the fur trade, international rivalry for colonies, adventurism, and the desire to gather useful information. The Enlightenment fostered in western Europe and the United States an ardent quest to collect, describe, and interpret the world. Resulting activities included charting unmapped coastlines and river courses, collecting specimens of flora and fauna, observing the lifeways of native peoples, and developing comparative word lists. The Lewis and Clark Expedition as well as the voy-ages of Cook, Vancouver, and others carried out these assignments.

The last partial spiral on the column dealt with the arrival of overland emigrants in the 1840s and–

Left: Artist Pusteria and crew completing the spiral mural, October 1926 (Oregon Historical Society Neg. No. 10138)

almost as an appendage–completion of railroad linkages in 1893 to the mouth of the Columbia River. Between 1843 and 1850 nearly 10,000 emigrants crossed the Oregon Trail. Their numbers increased steadily, and in 1859, Oregon gained statehood. From modest beginnings in 1860, the region devel-oped a railroad network, achieving transcontinental ties in 1883. Over the next three decades the rail-road network spread throughout the region with connecting lines to Astoria, Tillamook, Coos Bay, and other points for shipment of raw materials and manufactured goods.

The Astoria Column's murals represented the tri-umph of Euro-American sovereignty. Pusterla did not address the demographic calamity that befell Native Americans, their dispossession, or the ecological changes brought by the newcomers. He celebrated the development of a continental nation, the conse-quence of discovery, exploration, and settlement.

The cavalcade of history etched by the masterful Italian-American artist included several topics:

BEFORE THE WHITE PEOPLE ARRIVE

This scene, located closest to the column's base, depicts the forest primeval with the beaver, a key element in the fur trade, and other wildlife. The absence of Native Americans is notable since they had occupied the region for at least 10,000 years.

CAPTAIN ROBERT GRAY, SHIP COLUMBIA IN THE GREAT RIVER

The *Columbia Rediviva* was the first large vessel to cross over the bar of the Columbia. A trader working under a sea letter issued by President George Washington, Gray named the river for his ship. His "discovery" in 1792 became the foundation of American claims to the region.

*"*The fact that the events to be commemorated were those of peaceful rather than war time character made them if anything more worthwhile." Ralph Budd to C. M. Hyskell, December 1929

FIRST CONTACT: THE CHINOOK AND CLATSOP INDIANS

In 1792 Captain Robert Gray dropped anchor and began trading for salmon and furs with the Chinook and Clatsop tribes living at the entrance to the Columbia River. The Indians had for centuries bartered commodities of the shoreline for those of the interior. Maritime fur traders brought new commodities: blankets, cotton cloth, tools, firearms, beads, mirrors, and alcohol.

LIEUTENANT WILLIAM R. BROUGHTON NAMES MOUNT HOOD

Learning of Gray's "discovery," the British Captain George Vancouver dispatched his associate, Lieutenant Broughton, to examine the Columbia River in 1792. Broughton outfitted two whaleboats and made a reconnaissance to the head of tidewater. He sighted Mount Hood, naming it for Samuel Hood, a rear admiral in the British navy during the American Revolutionary War. Broughton's explorations helped fix British claims.

LEWIS AND CLARK EXPEDITION CROSSES THE MOUNTAINS

In both their westbound and eastbound travels, the Corps of Discovery confronted inclement weather, near-starvation, and great tribulation in the Bitterroot Mountains, part of the broad chain known as the Rockies.

INDIANS GREET THE EXPLORERS

For millennia, the mouth of the Columbia had been the homeland of the Clatsop and Chinook tribes. Sharing a common dialect of Lower Chinookan, these people were the wealthy traders at the mouth of the great river. They controlled precontact trade and, for a time, remained arbiters in the emerging fur trade.

LEWIS AND CLARK EXPEDITION REACHES THE PACIFIC

In November 1805, the Corps of Discovery examined the north shore of the Columbia from its base, Station Camp. After a reconnaissance of Cape Disappointment and a polling of the party, Captains Lewis and Clark decided to spend the winter on the south side of the river.

SALT WORKS ON THE PACIFIC SHORE

Having killed dozens of elk, the members of the Corps of Discovery confronted a major problem in preserving their food for the winter and the return journey. Captains Lewis and Clark dispatched a patrol to the seacoast to boil saltwater, extracting the salt for use in preserving the meat at Fort Clatsop.

FORT CLATSOP

Members of the Corps of Discovery spent nearly four weeks felling trees, splitting boards, and building their winter encampment on the banks of the Lewis and Clark River. The fort was the first U.S. Army post in the Pacific Northwest and was occupied from December 1805 to April 1806.

EXPLORERS COMPLETE FORT CLATSOP

The Lewis and Clark Expedition moved into Fort Clatsop on Christmas Day, 1805. The party faced a terrible, rainy winter. Hunting parties ranged through the countryside to kill elk and deer. Some of the men made candles, moccasins, and leather pantaloons for their return journey.

INDIAN FISHING AND CANOE-MAKING

The Chinookans were masterful makers of dugout canoes. Their large, sleek craft could carry several tons and cut through the choppy waters of the Columbia estuary. The Indians fished for salmon, sturgeon, steelhead, smelt, and lamprey eels.

ASTOR OVERLAND PARTY LEAVES ST. LOUIS

In 1810 John Jacob Astor, principal investor in the Pacific Fur Company, dispatched an overland party from St. Louis under Wilson Price Hunt, a company employee. The expedition reached Council Bluffs on the Missouri and then set out on horseback across the plains via the Platte River in July 1811.

Right: Pusteria's template for the historical murals, 1926

CCHS #3392-921, 3394-921

14

"The carving is quite shallow and cannot be classed as bas-relief."

Astoria Evening Budget, July 1, 1926

TONQUIN SAILS FROM NEW YORK

Bound for the mouth of the Columbia, the *Tonquin* sailed from New York City in September 1810 carrying seamen, workers, and supplies for Astor's fur-trading post on the Pacific coast. The *Tonquin* traveled around Cape Horn.

TONQUIN ARRIVES AT THE COLUMBIA

After a six-month voyage, including a two-week stay in the Hawaiian Islands, the *Tonquin* arrived in March 1811 at the entrance to the Columbia River. Its contentious captain, Jonathan Thorn, four times sent out men to sound the channel–eight drowned in the effort.

OVERLAND ASTORIANS CROSS THE DIVIDE

Enduring great adversity in the mountains, the party led by William Price Hunt followed the Snake River westward and nearly perished in 1812 in the Blue Mountains of eastern Oregon.

DESTRUCTION OF THE TONQUIN

In the summer of 1811, Captain Thorn took his vessel out of the Columbia and sailed north to trade for furs with the Indians. Although the story is unclear, the captain apparently antagonized the natives, who stormed the vessel. The ship blew up or sank with a loss of 27 people, probably on the west coast of Vancouver Island.

FIRST OVERLAND ASTORIANS ARRIVE

After 18 months in the field, most of Wilson Price Hunt's expedition reached Astoria in February 1812. Of 62 in the party, only 2 had died in the challenging trip across the American West.

THE LOST ASTORIANS

Ramsay Crooks and John Day, members of the overland party under Wilson Price Hunt, did not reach Astoria until May 1812. The men had lost almost everything but their lives.

TRANSFER OF ASTORIA TO THE NORTHWEST COMPANY

Having learned of the outbreak of a second war with Great Britain, later known as the War of 1812, John Jacob Astor's partners feared that the British navy might sail into the Columbia River and seize their fort. In October 1813, the "partners in the field" in Oregon dissolved the Pacific Fur Company and sold out to the Canadian-based North West Company of Montreal.

U.S. SHIP ONTARIO

By the term "status ante bellum" in the Treaty of Ghent (1814), which ended the War of 1812, the United States assumed no loss of its "discovery rights" to the Pacific Northwest. In 1818, Captain James Biddle sailed into the Columbia on the U.S. Navy vessel *Ontario* and symbolically took possession of both shores for the United States.

COMING OF THE PIONEERS

With the establishment of American Protestant missions to the Indians in 1834 and 1836, the stage was set to publicize the good soil, timber, fish, and climate of the Oregon Country. By 1850, more than 10,000 American citizens had emigrated overland to Oregon.

ARRIVAL OF THE RAILROAD IN ASTORIA

In the mid-1880s, railroad lines connected the Pacific Northwest to the rest of the continent. In 1893 the Seashore Railroad Company, later the Astoria & Columbia River Railroad, began a rail system at the mouth of the Columbia. Later the Great Northern acquired this line.

Although he was not a resident and lacked knowledge of Pacific Northwest history and Native American cultures, Pusterla accurately re-created most of the scenes illustrating major points in the region's early history. He etched powerful images showing the Native Americans, their housing, and the maritime fur traders. A few elements of the murals, however, were problematic: the depiction of Lewis and Clark arriving in ribbed boats (not dugouts), the appearance of Fort Clatsop (not founded on Clark's floor plan of the post), and the inclusion of totem poles where they did not exist.

RESTORING THE ASTORIA COLUMN

WITHIN THREE YEARS OF THE COLUMN'S COMPLETION, THE WIND AND RAIN RAKING COXCOMB HILL HAD TAKEN AN EVIDENT TOLL ON THE SGRAFFITO MURAL. WHILE THE TECHNIQUE FARED WELL IN MEDITERRANEAN CLIMATES OR CHURCH INTERIORS, THE RAVAGES OF UP TO 80 INCHES OF RAINFALL A YEAR AND THE DRIVING, SOUTHWESTERLY GALES SWEEPING OFF THE PACIFIC OCEAN DIMMED THE BEAUTY AND THREATENED THE CARVINGS ON THE GREAT SPIRALING MURAL OF HISTORY ETCHED BY PUSTERLA.

The onset of the Great Depression in October 1929 crushed fund-raising efforts. The future of the column's artwork looked bleak in spite of civic support. Litchfield told city officials that Pusterla was the only man who could stabilize the mural, but the estimated cost of $5,000 seemed unobtainable. Pusterla had, in the meantime, received a major commission to create a series of murals and decorate the dome of the New York County Courthouse. He had completed sketches for the dome in 1927, but the project remained unfunded until it was adopted as a public art project under the Works Progress Administration. In 1934, Pusterla and his assistants began nearly two years of work on the rotunda mural illustrating the history of law in scenes with more than 300 figures.

While the artist was busily employed in New York City, the Astor family offered $3,000, the Great Northern Railway gave $500, and the city, drawing from taxes, budgeted $2,000. With scaffolding in place, Pusterla returned to Astoria in July 1936 to repair damage and waterproof the mural. The artist, then 74 years old, was assisted by Charles Ettro of Astoria and Daniel Billoresi of New York. The team began by washing the column with hydrochloric acid to counter its discoloration. They then coated the mural with dehydratine, a chemical used for waterproofing concrete and masonry. The plan was to treat the mural with this material at five-year intervals.

Pusterla died in 1941. The Astoria Column was among his most notable works, as evidenced by the nearly 22,000 tourists who visited the landmark that year.

During World War II the site was closed to the public. The U.S. Navy, which had a large facility at nearby Tongue Point and a blimp squadron for coastal reconnaissance at the Tillamook Naval Air Station, controlled Coxcomb Hill and used it for a navigational air facility. The column reopened to the public in 1947. The following year, Earl G. Griffith, a painting contractor, descended the column in a bosun's chair to spray it with tung oil, the first treatment in years. City workers treated it again in 1958. The waterproofing created problems: it accentuated differences in the 1926 and 1936 *sgraffito*, darkened the colors, and trapped dirt and lichen.

By 1968 the column had developed a number of problems, including cracks on its surface and fading in the murals. In an effort to mitigate the damage, workers used a bright white latex paint to revitalize the wreath and egg-and-dart moldings at the top of the column and the medallions found in the spiraling murals. The project ignored the *sgraffito* lines and further diminished the portraiture in the medallions. Meriwether Lewis, in fact, acquired lambchop sideburns as a consequence of this work.

To deal with the cracks, workers injected epoxy grout, but, because of expansion and contraction, the epoxy did not hold. Furthermore, X-rays confirmed that the concrete column was supported only by wire mesh. In 1976, the city closed the column so workers could install metal rings—set about a foot apart and joined with vertical steel rods—inside the column. The crew replaced electrical wiring and sandblasted the interior.

"This magnificent column deserved to be restored. Therefore, we searched for the right consultants to guide this effort. By retaining Frank Preusser we were confident the restoration would be successful and this legacy preserved for generations to come."

Jordan D. Schnitzer, President, Friends of Astoria Column

Above: Stages of conservation project, 1994-95

Years passed and the great exterior mural continued to deteriorate, faded and worn by time and the elements. A chance conversation between Jordan Schnitzer, a Portland philanthropist whose family roots were in Astoria, with then-Mayor Edith Henningsgaard, spurred determination to save the column. In 1984, the City of Astoria, led by the mayor with strong support of council members such as Duncan Law, budgeted $75,000 in the last year of the Federal Revenue Sharing Program for restoration work on the column. Fred Lindstrom, head of Astoria's Parks and Recreation Division, began investigation into restoration prospects. The concern of these citizens led in 1988 to the creation of a private, nonprofit organization, Friends of Astoria Column, Inc. This group sought to broaden public interest in the column and to raise the necessary money to restore the monument and its surrounding grounds.

In 1989 the Friends hired Myrna Saxe Conservators, Art and Architecture, to clean the exterior of the column by removing tung oil, lichens, and dirt. Project workers scrubbed the column with toothbrushes. The process worked, in part, but the murals were so dimmed by the ravages of weather and time that Pusterla's *sgraffito*

artistry appeared to face a limited and cloudy future.

Aware that the Astoria Column was in jeopardy, Friends of Astoria Column renewed its goal and ultimately raised more than $1,000,000, including $700,000 in hard funds, to restore the column, preserve as much of Pusterla's artistry as possible, and extend the life of the structure. The efforts culminated in 1994-95 when the J. Paul Getty Museum, in Los Angeles, suggested retaining the services of Frank Preusser. A world-renowned art conservator who had worked on the Sphinx in Egypt and the Angkor Wat temples in Cambodia, among other projects, Preusser enjoyed taking on challenges. Both he and Schnitzer were convinced that the column, though not as old as other antiquities, was equally worthy of preservation.

In 1995, Preusser arrived in Astoria and, working with a local crew, mounted a major project. Workers enclosed the column in scaffolding and wrapped that with plastic to protect the conservators from the weather. Working in their vast plastic cocoon, Preusser's artists began the challenging task of bringing new life to Pusterla's murals. Although it was the newest artwork he had contracted to

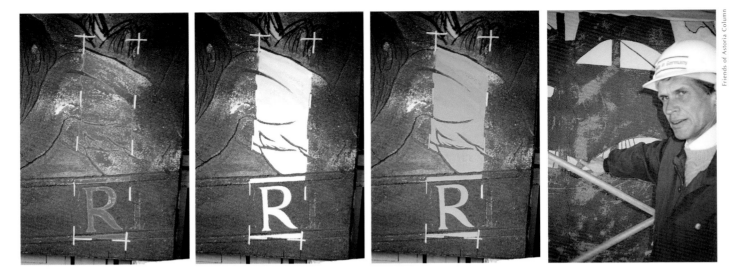

Friends of Astoria Column

restore, Preusser said, "I find a genuine need for people to know where they come from, for people to look in the past to find and be proud of past achievement and have hope for the future. We are the transition between past and future. If we destroy the past, where do we come from? Where's our point of reference?"

Preusser's team of conservators, including student interns, used historical photographs and the original scratch lines to restore the murals. The challenge was great, for only an estimated 20 percent of the art remained when they began the project. When the work was completed, the crew treated the column with siloxane-based water repellent. Preusser recommended reapplications every 8 to 15 years.

The "pillar of the community" in Astoria clearly had a brighter future when the scaffolding came down in November 1995 and the Astoria Column again greeted visitors. The 1995 restoration also included rebuilding the column's doors of Alaska cedar, restoring the cupola and cleaning its windows, and replacing the long-vanished copper finial that once stood atop the column. The City of Astoria replaced the railing on the viewing platform, replicating the original iron balustrade in stainless steel and also meeting modern building codes.

By the beginning of the 21st century the throngs who annually visited the Astoria Column had grown from the tens of thousands to the hundreds of thousands. Coxcomb Hill offered distinctive attractions: a panoramic view in a city park setting and, most of all, the remarkable Astoria Column.

Ralph Budd's dream of creating symbols to remind Americans of their history had attained its greatest success at precisely the point he and city leaders felt had the most potential. The Astoria Column had become a monument to the deeds and lore of former generations for the consideration of the present. Thomas Jefferson had stated matters correctly when he observed, "The earth is for the living." And Ralph Budd might well have added, "provided they remember their past."

FRIENDS OF ASTORIA COLUMN

Preservation efforts require broad bases of support. Those seeking to preserve and restore the Astoria Column have forged special public-private cooperation. The City of Astoria and its officials, led initially by Mayor Edith Henningsgaard and now by Mayor Willis Van Dusen, have worked side by side with citizens from throughout Oregon and elsewhere to chart a program, raise money, and mount the restoration agenda in Astor Park on Coxcomb Hill. The mission of the advocacy group is to document the column's significance, seek its restoration and preservation, and provide educational experiences for visitors.

Fund-raising has been central to the work of the Friends of Astoria Column. The Astoria Column has many needs: conservation of its murals, seismic upgrades and stabilization of its base, redesign of traffic flow and pedestrian access, improved accessibility to meet the standards of the Americans with Disabilities Act, improving the landscaping, introducing flora native to the site, providing permanent exterior night lighting of the column, and upgrading the site's infrastructure with a new water line, sewer connection, and overflow parking lot.

The investment of time and resources of the Friends of Astoria Column has yielded some wonderful results, most notably the restoration of the *sgraffito* murals, column doors, cupola, and finial in 1994-95. Lord Astor of Hever, a descendant of John Jacob Astor, is but one who has helped in this cause. The commitment of residents of Astoria, Oregonians, and others to the monument helps the Friends organization achieve its objectives. The task is not done. Challenges remain. The dedicated members of the Friends of Astoria Column eagerly look forward to achieving more of their objectives and furthering the group's educational mission.

Above: Detailed view of restoration work, 1994-95. Frank Preusser, world-renowned art conservator, working with a local crew including student interns, used historical photographs, original drawings, and scratch lines to restore Pusterla's murals.
Right: New ADA-accessible granite walkway leading to the column. A map orients visitors to nearby sites and geographical features.

TIMELINE

1898 Astoria Progressive Commercial Commission plans an observatory for Coxcomb Hill

1911 Astoria Centennial Committee erects an electric sign on Coxcomb Hill

1912 City of Astoria purchases parkland on Coxcomb Hill

1917 Tree/flagpole created on Coxcomb Hill

1923 Lightning destroys tree/flagpole on Coxcomb Hill

1925 Ralph Budd conceives landmark to honor early explorers at the mouth of the Columbia River

1926 January: Electus D. Litchfield designs the Astoria Column
March: Crews clear the construction site
April: Concrete poured
June: Attilio Pusterla, artist, completes mural designs
July 22: Astoria Column dedicated
October: *Sgraffito* mural completed

1936 Attilio Pusterla restores mural and coats it

1942 Astoria Column closed because of World War II

1947 Astoria Column reopened

1948 City of Astoria treats mural with tung oil

1958 City of Astoria treats mural with tung oil

1968 Mural repainted and epoxy inserted in column cracks

1974 Astoria Column listed in the National Register of Historic Places

1976 Steel rings and rods installed inside Astoria Column

1988 Friends of Astoria Column founded

1989 Mural cleaned and stabilized

1995 Frank Preusser mounts mural restoration project; Astoria Column doors, cupola, and finial restored and repaired

Friends of Astoria Column, Inc.
P.O. Box 717
Astoria, Oregon 97103
503-325-2963

City of Astoria
Mayor Willis L. Van Dusen

Friends of Astoria Column, Inc.
President Jordan D. Schnitzer

Board of Directors
Jon Englund
Michael Foster
Bill Hall
Mike Lindberg
Edith Henningsgaard-Miller
Susan Sandoz Miller
Eric Paulson
Cheryl Perrin
Christine Powers
Ruth Shaner
Hal Snow
Thane Tienson
Gayle Timmerman
Chester Trabucco
Karen Whitman
Board Liaison Kandis Brewer Nunn

Sources Consulted
Articles and Pamphlets

Daily Astorian. *Monumental Restoration: The History and Restoration of the Astoria Column.* Astoria, Oregon: The Daily Astorian, 1995.

Evans, Gail. Astoria Column, National Historic Landmark Nomination. State Historic Preservation Office, Salem, Oregon, 1997.

Fransen, Joean K. "The Astoria Column," *Cumtux: Clatsop County Historical Society Quarterly,* 16(4)(Fall 1996):2-17.

Great Northern Railway. *Program of Columbia River Historical Expedition, July 15-27, 1926.* St. Paul, Minnesota: Great Northern Railway, 1926.

Kimbrell, Leonard B. "Some New Light on the Astoria Column." In *Festschrift.* N.p., Northern Pacific Coast Chapter, Society of Architectural Historians, 1978, 51-55.

Potter, Elisabeth Walton. "The Missionary and Immigrant Experience as Portrayed in Commemorative Works of Art," *Idaho Yesterdays* 31 (Spring/Summer 1987):95-116.

Newspapers

"The Astoria Column," *The Columbian* (Vancouver, Washington), August 2, 1995.

"Column Will Be Restored This Season," *Oregon Journal* (Portland, Oregon), February 24, 1936.

"Credit for Column Given Engineers and Architect," *The Oregonian* (Portland, Oregon), July 25, 1926.

"First Carving on Astoria Column Is Started Today," *Astoria Evening Budget* (Astoria, Oregon), July 1, 1926.

"Historical Expedition Dedicates Huge Astoria Column," *The Sunday Oregonian* (Portland, Oregon), July 25, 1926.

"Interpreting a Pillar of the Community," *The Oregonian* (Portland, Oregon), October 22, 2003.

"Noble Monument to Cap Coxcomb Hill," *Astoria Evening Budget* (Astoria, Oregon), February 24, 1926.

"Restoration Returns Pillar of Community," *The Register-Guard* (Eugene, Oregon), October 8, 1995.

"Work to Start Soon on Monument Site," *Astoria Evening Budget* (Astoria, Oregon), February 6, 1926.

International Standard Book Number 0-9759148-0-4
Text © 2004 Stephen Dow Beckham
Photography © 2004 Robert M. Reynolds
Book Design Reynolds Wulf Inc.
   Robert M. Reynolds, Letha Gibbs Wulf
Typography Letha Gibbs Wulf
Editor Judy McNally
Illustration Brett Reynolds
Printing Printing Today
Project Consultants Jordan D. Schnitzer, Kandis Brewer Nunn,
   Karen Whitman

Acknowledgments
Special thanks are extended to Liisa Penner and Lisa Studts, Clatsop County Historical Society; Sue Seyl, Photographs Curator, Oregon Historical Society; and Friends of Astoria Column photographers. Institutions providing photographs include the Clatsop County Historical Museum, Astoria; Oregon Historical Society, Portland; J. Paul Getty Museum, Los Angeles; and Newberry Library, Chicago.

Copyright 2004 by the Friends of Astoria Column, Inc.
All rights reserved.